HAL•LEONARD

GUITAR
PLAY-ALONG®

VOL. 123

LENNON *and* McCARTNEY *acoustic*

Guitar in cover photo courtesy of Cream City Music, Milwaukee, WI

ISBN 978-1-4234-9273-3

HAL•LEONARD®
CORPORATION
7777 W. BLUEMOUND RD. P.O. BOX 13819 MILWAUKEE, WI 53213

Visit Hal Leonard Online at
www.halleonard.com

CONTENTS

Guitar Notation Legend

THE MUSICAL STAFF shows pitches and rhythms and is divided by bar lines into measures. Pitches are named after the first seven letters of the alphabet.

TABLATURE graphically represents the guitar fingerboard. Each horizontal line represents a string, and each number represents a fret.

4th string, 2nd fret   1st & 2nd strings open, played together   open D chord

HALF-STEP BEND: Strike the note and bend up 1/2 step.

WHOLE-STEP BEND: Strike the note and bend up one step.

GRACE NOTE BEND: Strike the note and immediately bend up as indicated.

SLIGHT (MICROTONE) BEND: Strike the note and bend up 1/4 step.

BEND AND RELEASE: Strike the note and bend up as indicated, then release back to the original note. Only the first note is struck.

PRE-BEND: Bend the note as indicated, then strike it.

VIBRATO: The string is vibrated by rapidly bending and releasing the note with the fretting hand.

PALM MUTING: The note is partially muted by the pick hand lightly touching the string(s) just before the bridge.

HAMMER-ON: Strike the first (lower) note with one finger, then sound the higher note (on the same string) with another finger by fretting it without picking.

PULL-OFF: Place both fingers on the notes to be sounded. Strike the first note and without picking, pull the finger off to sound the second (lower) note.

LEGATO SLIDE: Strike the first note and then slide the same fret-hand finger up or down to the second note. The second note is not struck.

SHIFT SLIDE: Same as legato slide, except the second note is struck.

TRILL: Very rapidly alternate between the notes indicated by continuously hammering on and pulling off.

TAPPING: Hammer ("tap") the fret indicated with the pick-hand index or middle finger and pull off to the note fretted by the fret hand.

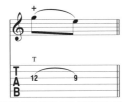

NATURAL HARMONIC: Strike the note while the fret-hand lightly touches the string directly over the fret indicated.

PINCH HARMONIC: The note is fretted normally and a harmonic is produced by adding the edge of the thumb or the tip of the index finger of the pick hand to the normal pick attack.

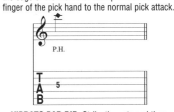

TREMOLO PICKING: The note is picked as rapidly and continuously as possible.

VIBRATO BAR DIVE AND RETURN: The pitch of the note or chord is dropped a specified number of steps (in rhythm), then returned to the original pitch.

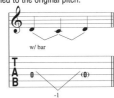

VIBRATO BAR SCOOP: Depress the bar just before striking the note, then quickly release the bar.

VIBRATO BAR DIP: Strike the note and then immediately drop a specified number of steps, then release back to the original pitch.

Additional Musical Definitions

   *(accent)*   • Accentuate note (play it louder).

   (staccato)   • Play the note short.

D.S. al Coda   • Go back to the sign (𝄋), then play until the measure marked "*To Coda*," then skip to the section labelled "**Coda**."

D.C. al Fine   • Go back to the beginning of the song and play until the measure marked "*Fine*" (end).

Fill   • Label used to identify a brief melodic figure which is to be inserted into the arrangement.

N.C.   • Harmony is implied.

   • Repeat measures between signs.

• When a repeated section has different endings, play the first ending only the first time and the second ending only the second time.

And I Love Her

Words and Music by John Lennon and Paul McCartney

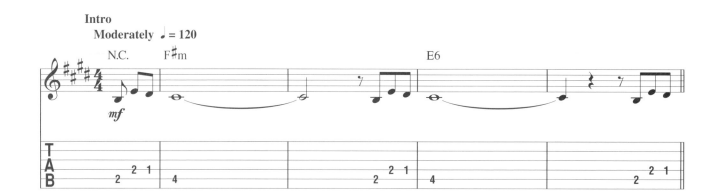

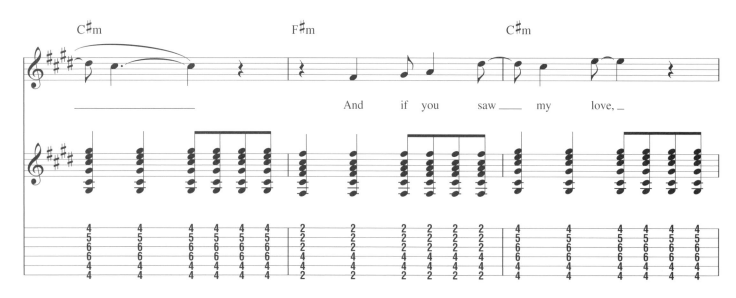

you'd love her too. _____ I _____ love _____ her. _____

% Verse

2nd time, substitute Fill 1

2. She gives me ev-'ry - thing, _____ and ten-der - ly. _____
3. *See additional lyrics*

The kiss my lov-er brings, _____

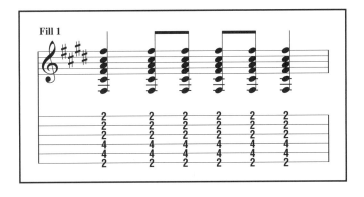

Fill 1

To Coda ⊕

she brings to me, and I love her.

Bridge

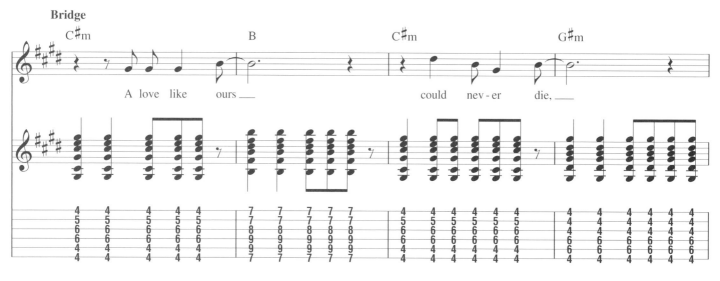

A love like ours could nev-er die,

D.S. al Coda

as long as I have you near me.

⊕ **Coda**

Guitar Solo

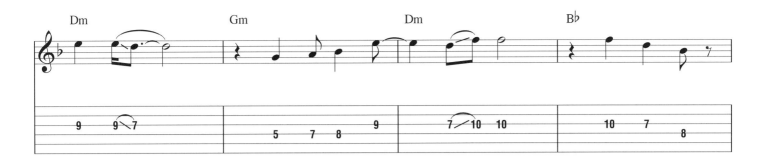

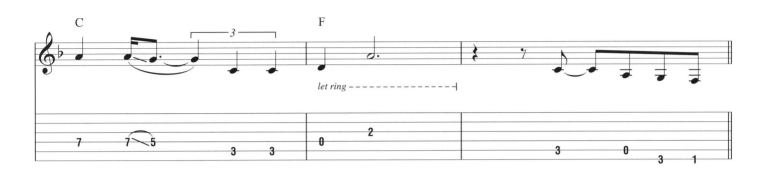

Verse

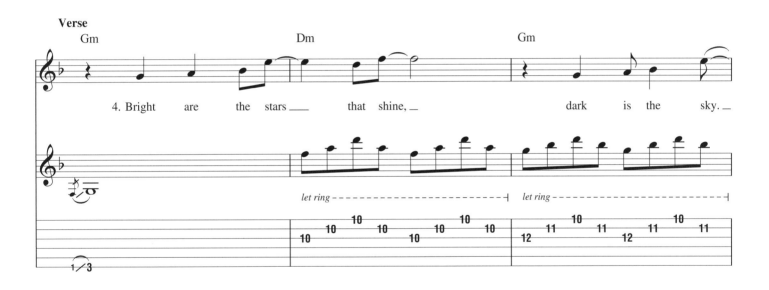

4. Bright are the stars ___ that shine, ___ dark is the sky. ___

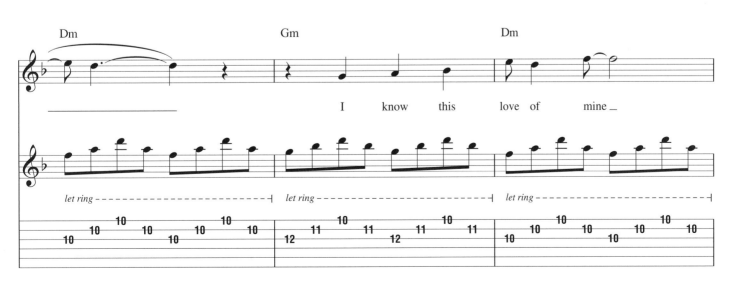

___ I know this love of mine ___

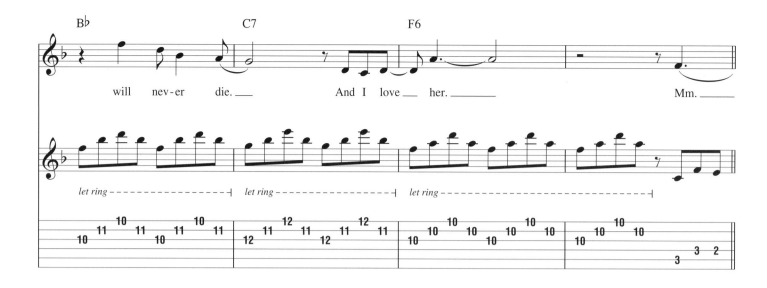

will nev-er die. ___ And I love ___ her. ___ Mm. ___

Outro

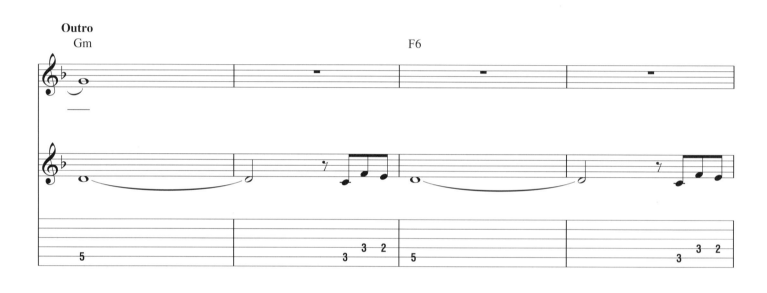

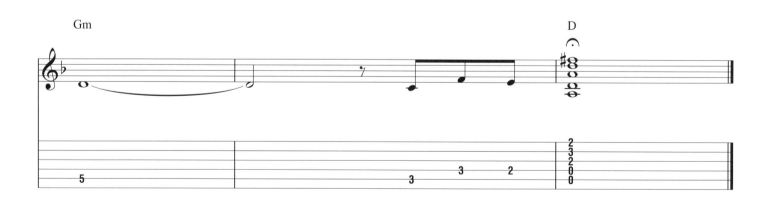

Additional Lyrics

3. Bright are the stars that shine,
   Dark is the sky.
   I know this love of mine
   Will never die, and I love her.

Help!

Words and Music by John Lennon and Paul McCartney

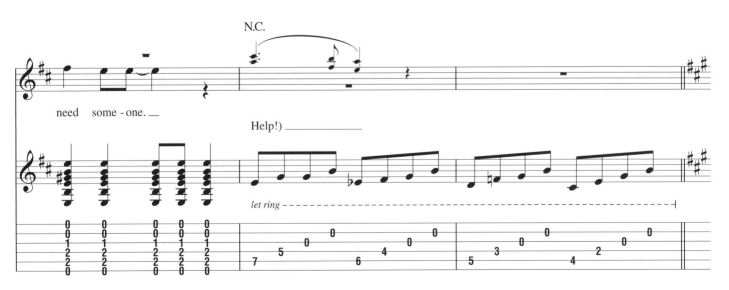

Verse

1. When I _____ was youn - ger, so _____ much
2. *See additional lyrics*

youn - ger than ___ to - day, _____ I nev - er need - ed

an - y - bod - y's help in an - y way. ___

But now these days are gone ___ and I'm not so self - as -

But now these days are gone _ and I'm not so self-as-sured. _____

D.S. al Coda

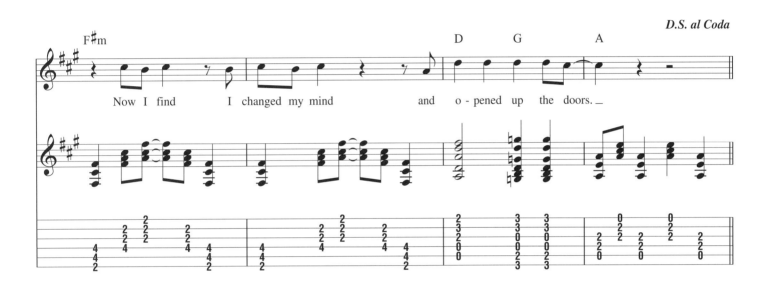

Now I find I changed my mind and o-pened up the doors. _

$\oplus$ **Coda**

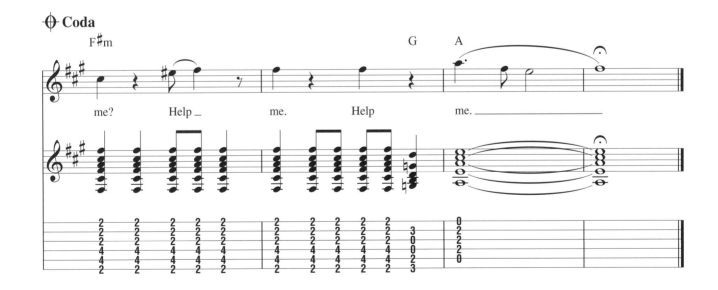

me? Help _ me. Help me. _____

Additional Lyrics

2. And now my life has changed in oh, so many ways.
My independence seems to vanish in the haze.
But every now and then I feel so insecure.
I know that I just need you like I've never done before.

Can't Buy Me Love

Words and Music by John Lennon and Paul McCartney

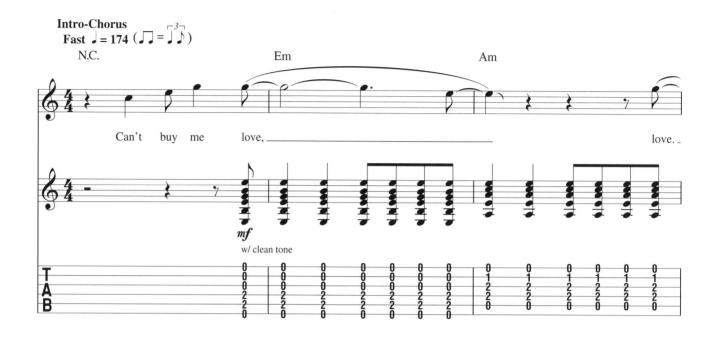

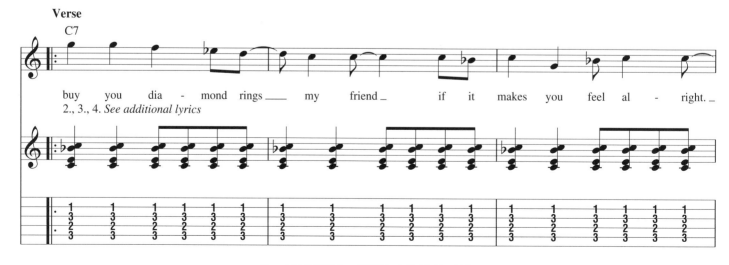

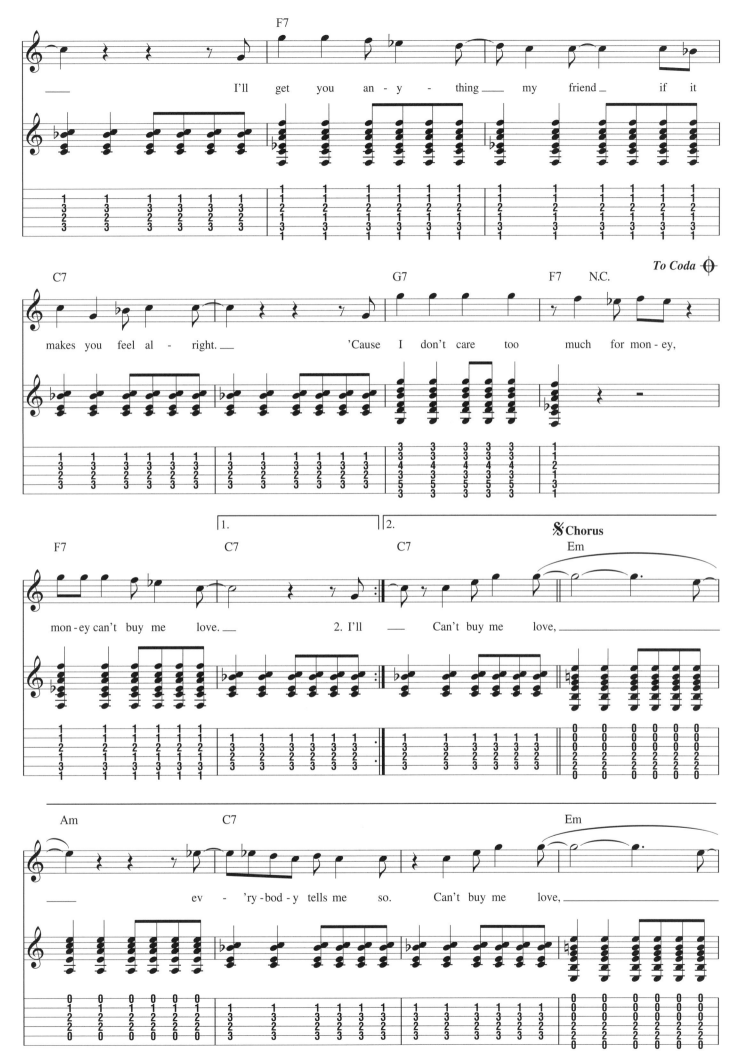

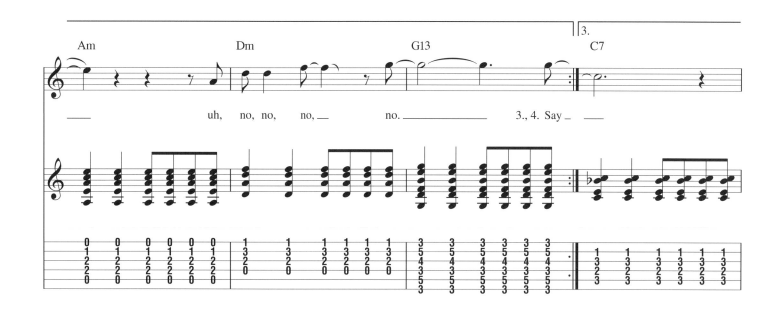

uh, no, no, no,___ no. _____ 3., 4. Say ___

Guitar Solo

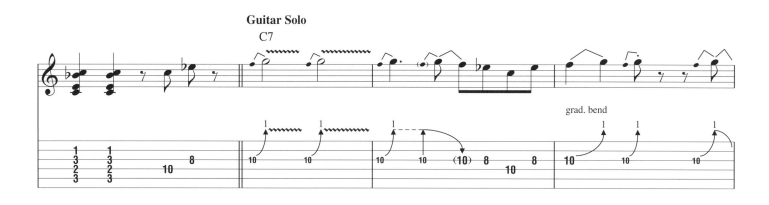

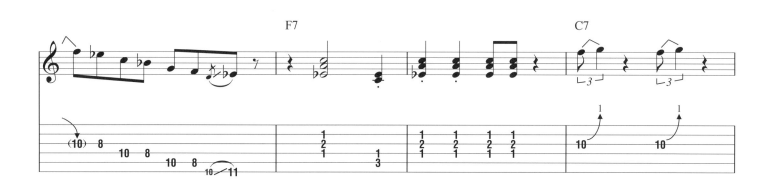

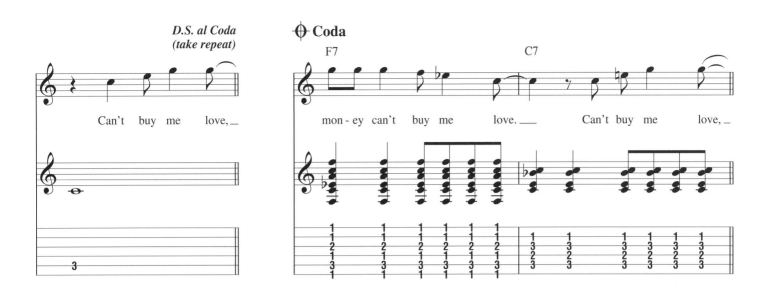

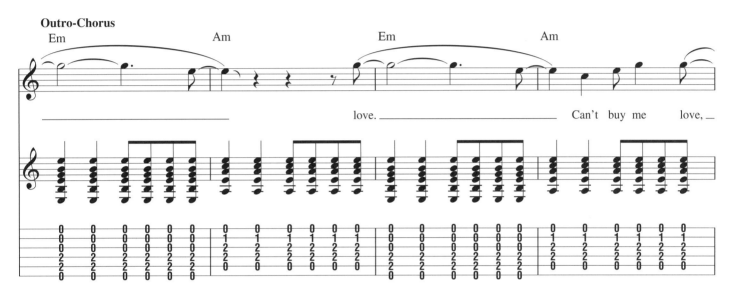

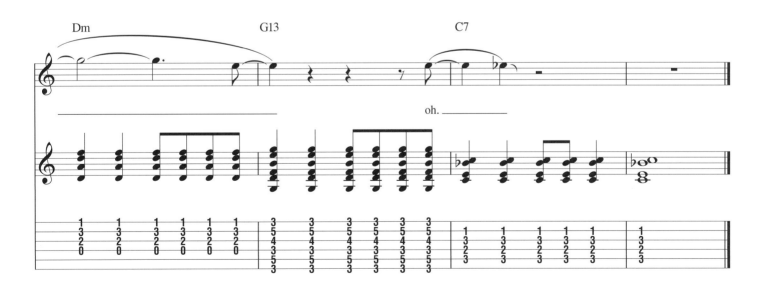

Additional Lyrics

2. I'll give you all I got to give if you say you love me too.
   I may not have a lot to give but what I got I'll give to you.
   I don't care too much for money, money can't buy me love.

3., 4. Say you don't need no diamond rings and I'll be satisfied.
   Tell me that you want the kind of things that money just can't buy.
   I don't care too much for money, money can't buy me love.

A Day in the Life

Words and Music by John Lennon and Paul McCartney

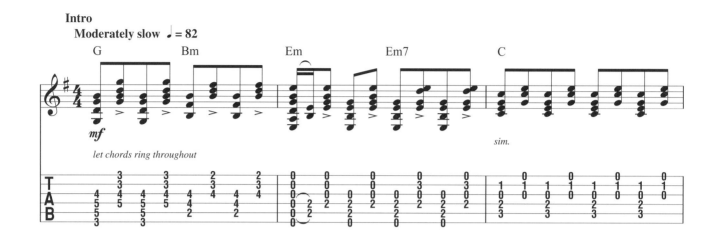

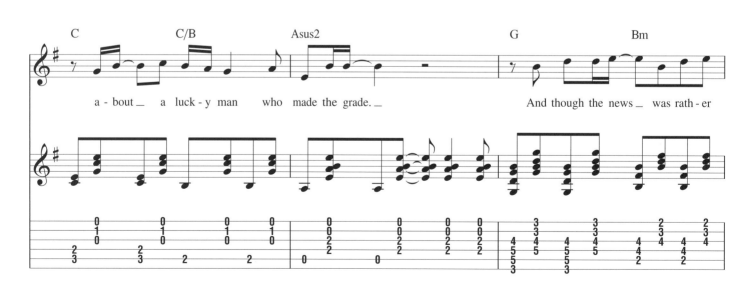

No-bod-y was real-ly sure if he was from the House of Lords.

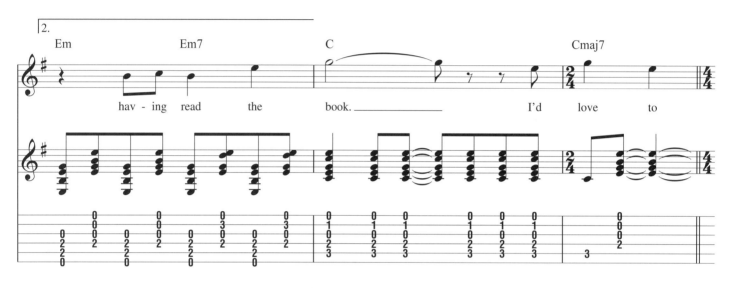

hav-ing read the book. I'd love to

Interlude
Double-time ♩ = 164

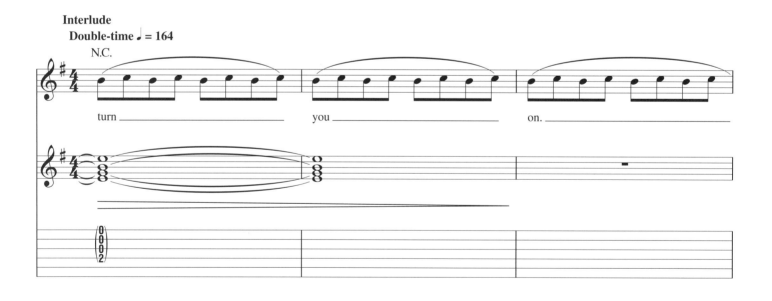

turn you on.

Gtr. tacet

20

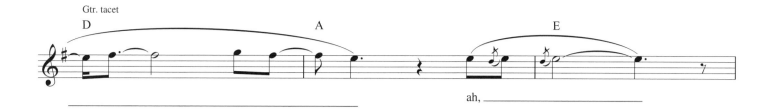

Verse
Double-time ♩ = 164

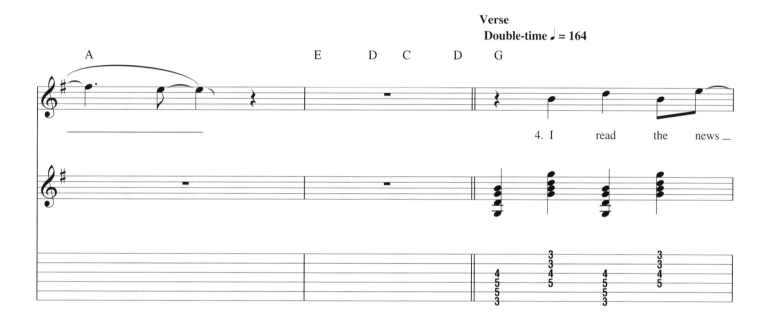

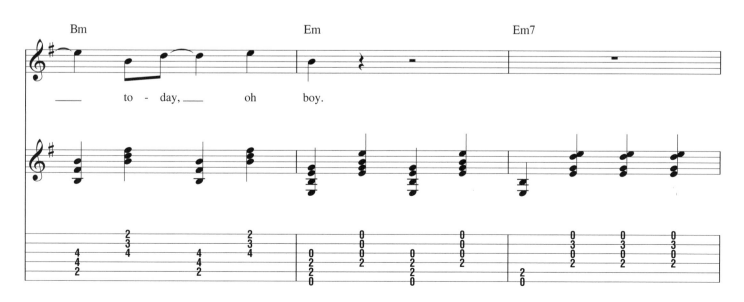

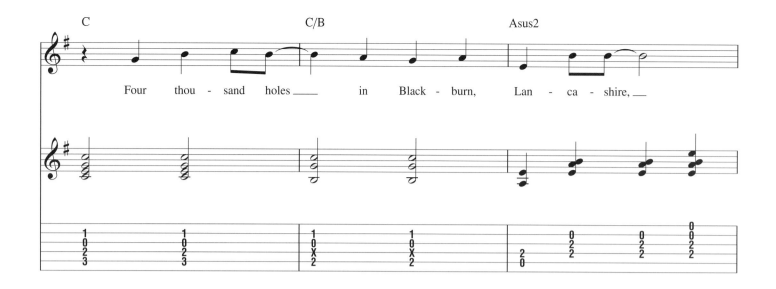

Four thou - sand holes ___ in Black - burn, Lan - ca - shire, ___

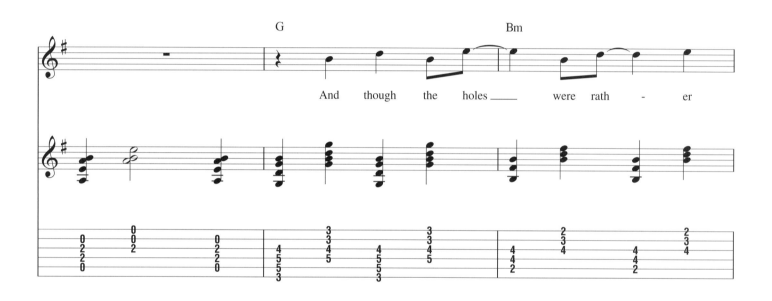

And though the holes ___ were rath - er

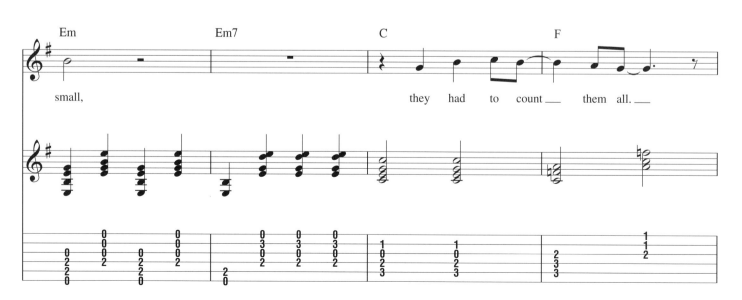

small, they had to count ___ them all. ___

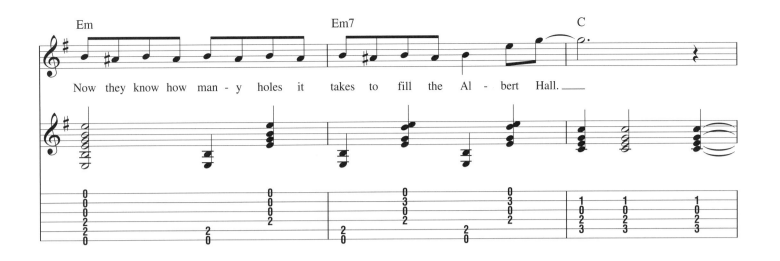

Now they know how man - y holes it takes to fill the Al - bert Hall. _____

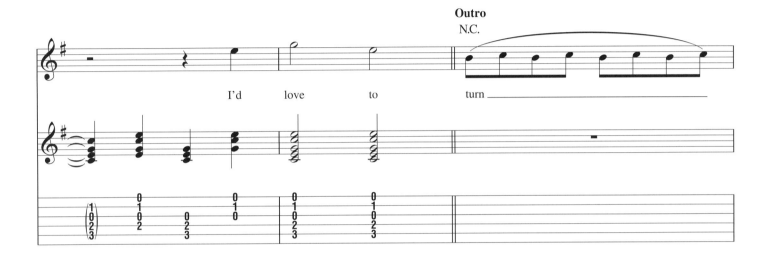

Outro

N.C.

I'd love to turn _____ you _____ on. _____

Gtr. tacet

Outro

Additional Lyrics

3. I saw a film today, oh boy.
   The English army had just won the war.
   A crowd of people turned away.
   But I just had to look, having read the book.

Eight Days a Week

Words and Music by John Lennon and Paul McCartney

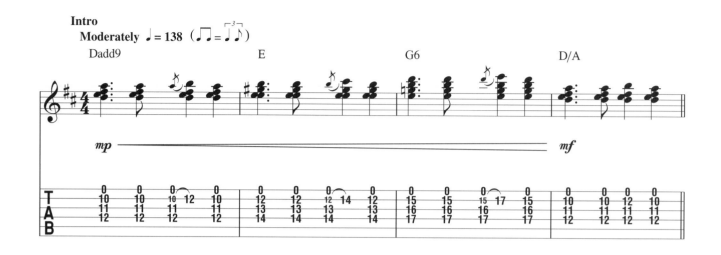

Intro
Moderately ♩ = 138

Dadd9   E   G6   D/A

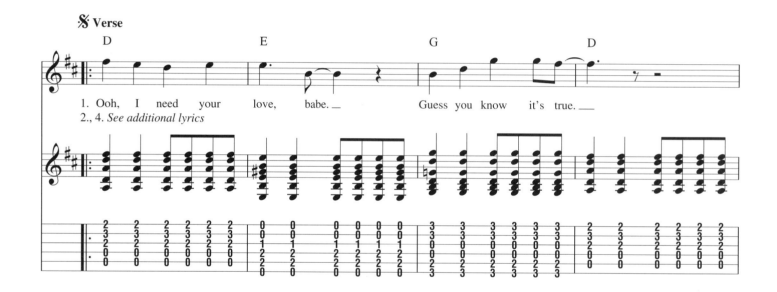

Verse

D   E   G   D

1. Ooh, I need your love, babe. __ Guess you know it's true. __
2., 4. *See additional lyrics*

E   G   D

Hope you need my love, babe, __ just like I need you. __

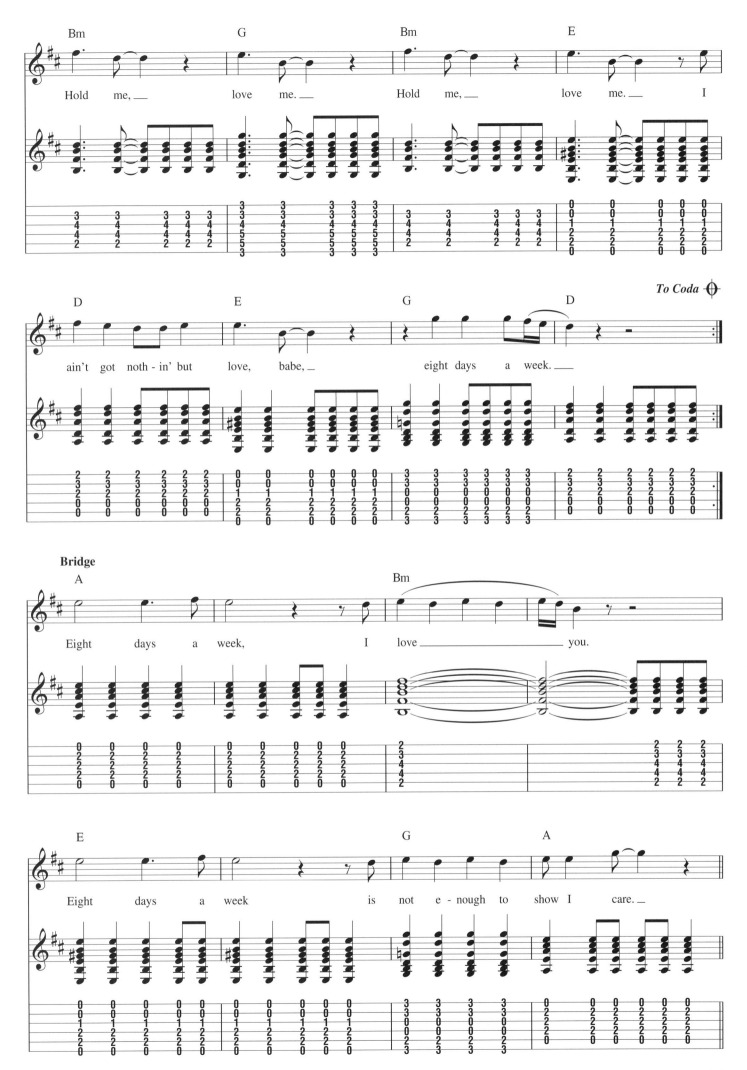

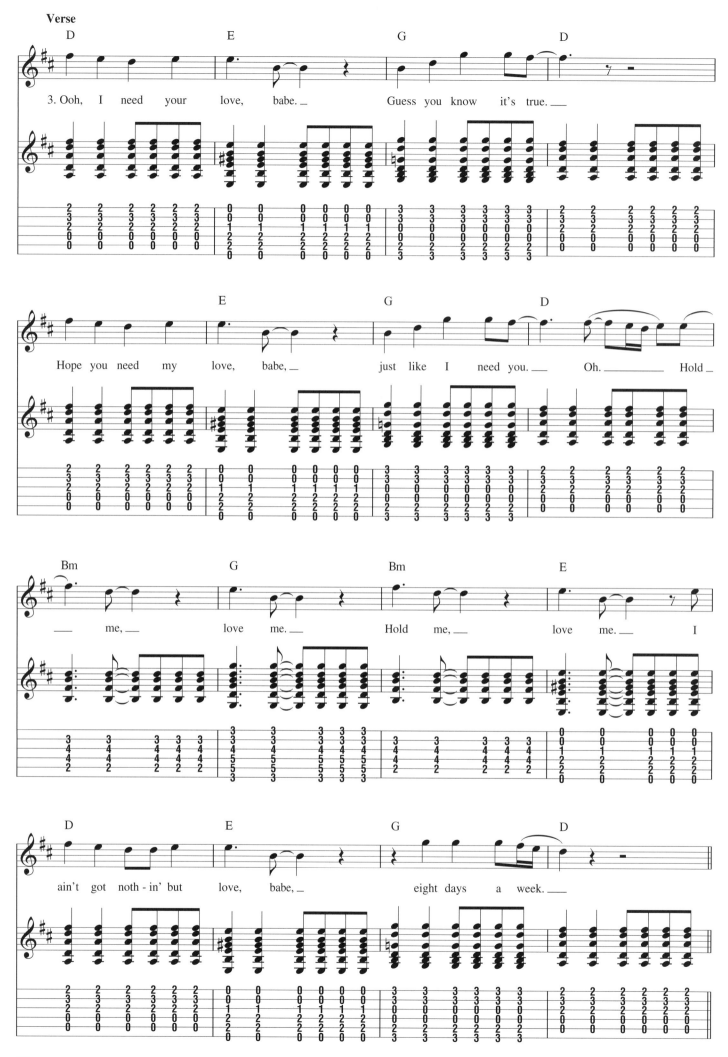

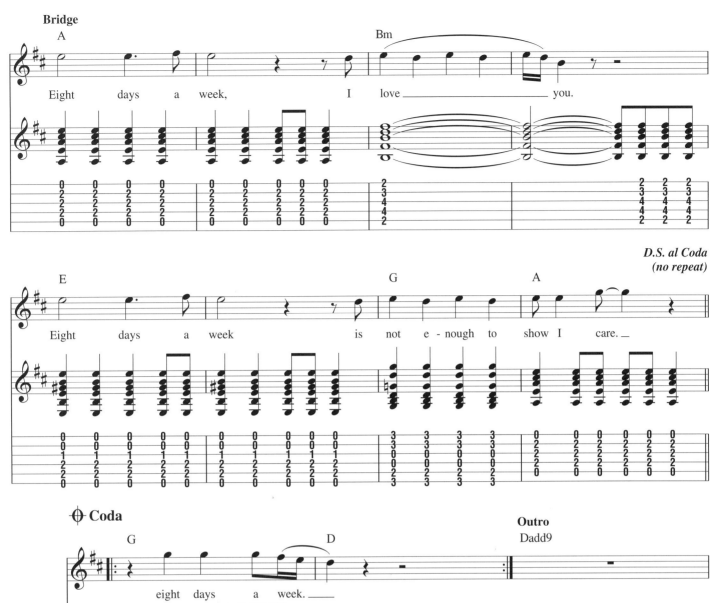

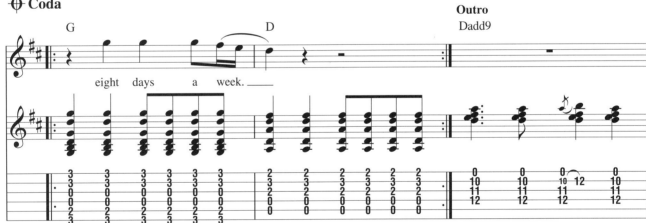

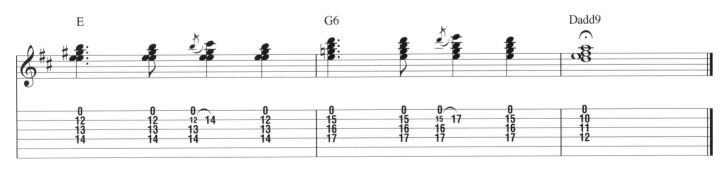

Additional Lyrics

2. Love you ev'ry day, girl,
   Always on my mind.
   One thing I can say, girl,
   Love you all the time.
   Hold me, love me.
   Hold me, love me.
   I ain't got nothin' but love, girl,
   Eight days a week.

4. Love you ev'ry day, girl,
   Always on my mind.
   One thing I can say, girl,
   Love you all the time.
   Hold me, love me.
   Hold me, love me.
   I ain't got nothin' but love, babe,
   Eight days a week.

Michelle

Words and Music by John Lennon and Paul McCartney

Capo V

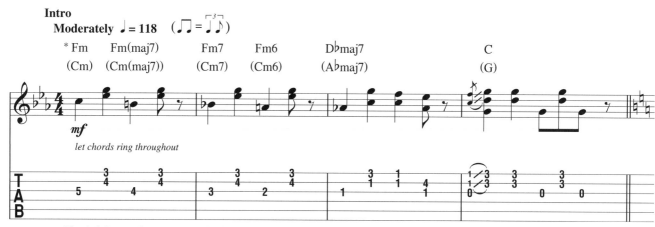

*Symbols in parentheses represent chord names respective to capoed guitars.
Symbols above reflect actual sounding chords. Capoed fret is "0" in tab.

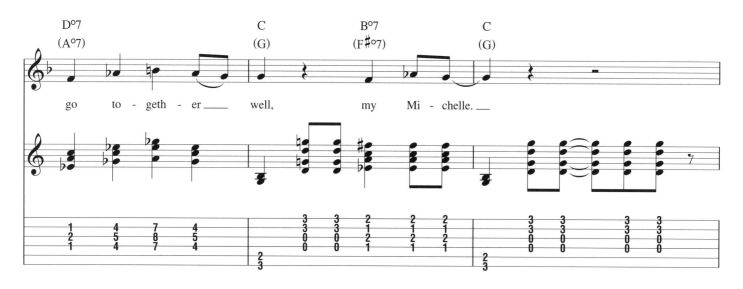

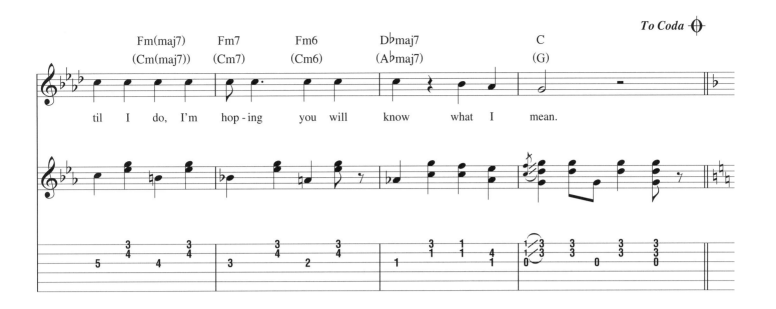

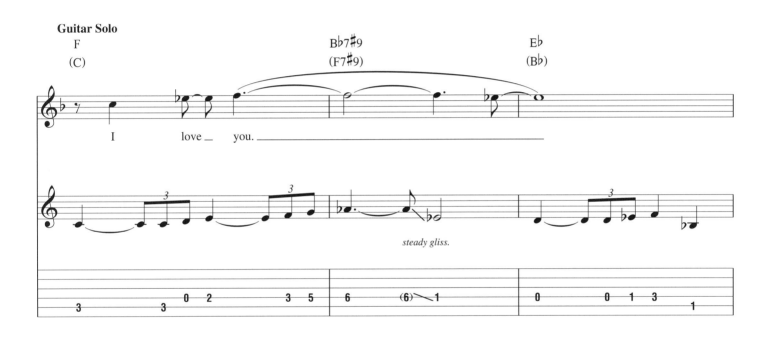

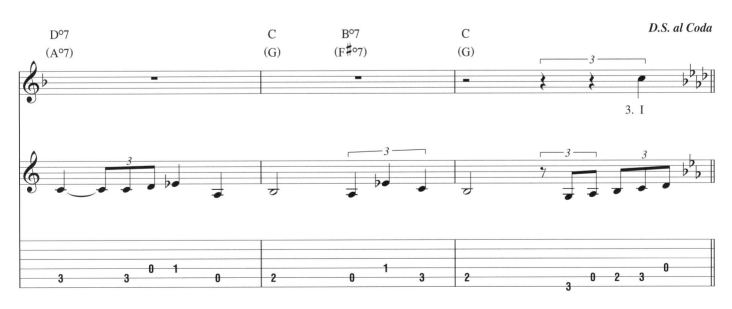

⊕ Coda
Chorus

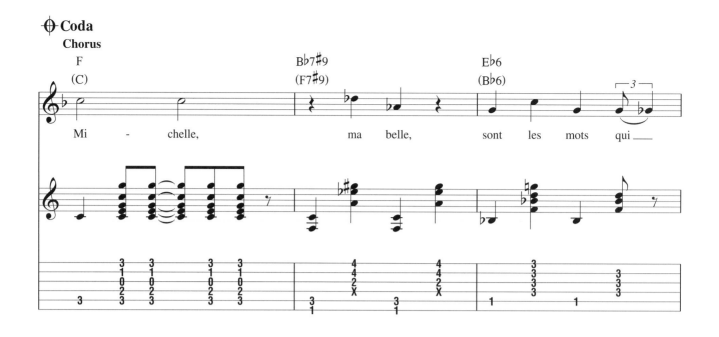

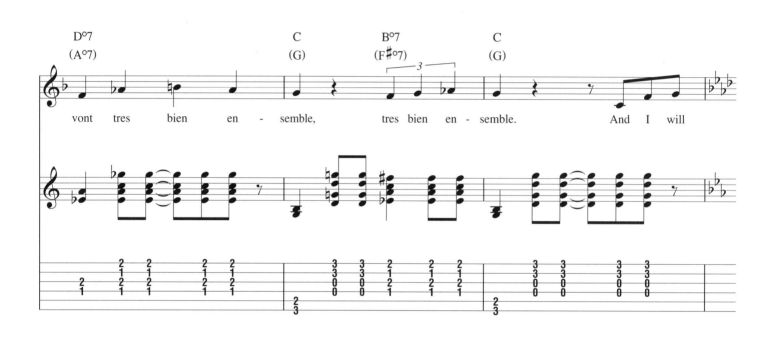

Outro

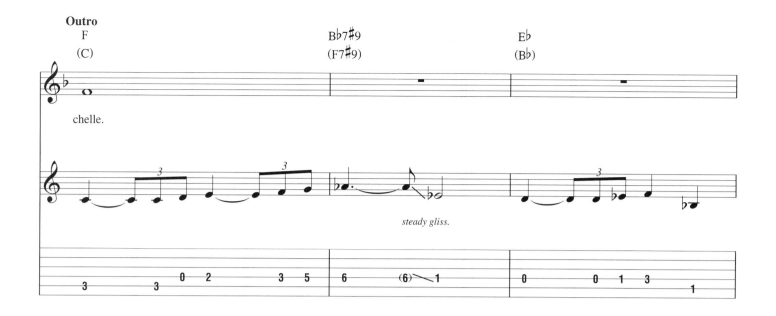

chelle.

steady gliss.

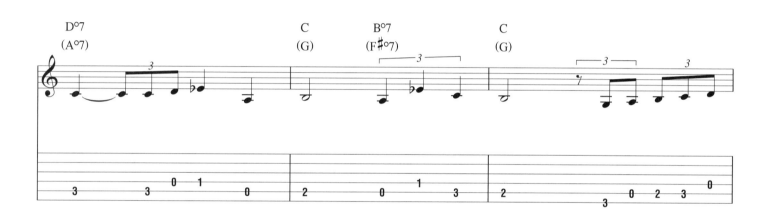

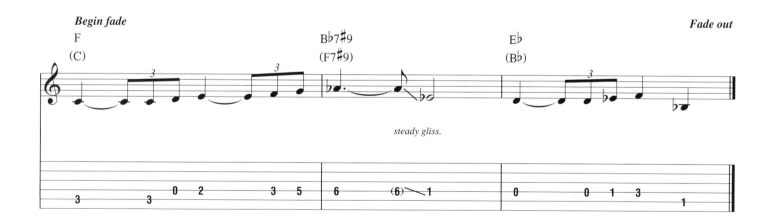

Begin fade

Fade out

steady gliss.

Additional Lyrics

3. I want you, I want you, I want you.
   I think you know by now.
   I'll get to you somehow.
   Until I do, I'm telling you so you'll understand.

We Can Work It Out

Words and Music by John Lennon and Paul McCartney

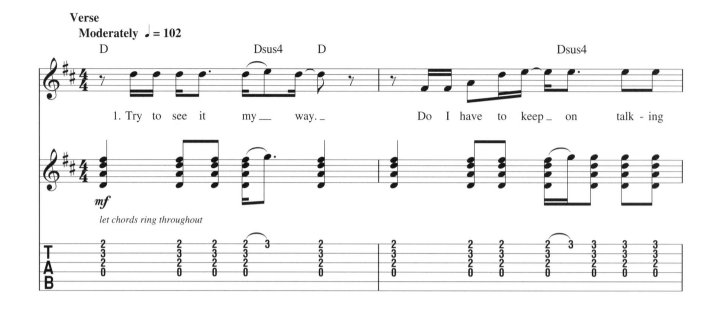

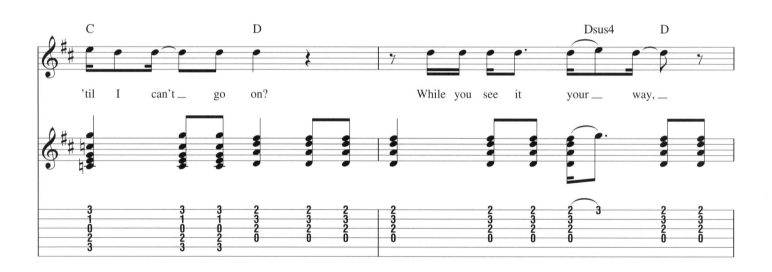

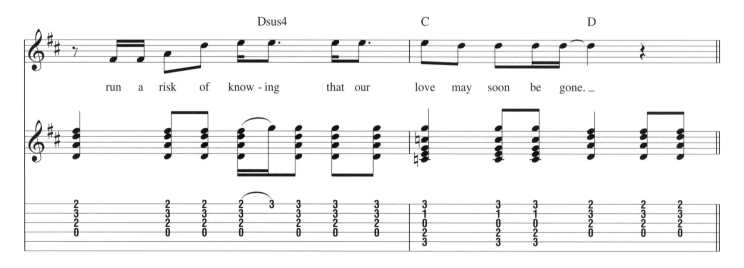

Additional Lyrics

3., 4. Try to see it my way.
Only time will tell if I am right or I am wrong.
While you see it your way,
There's a chance that we may fall apart before too long.

Yellow Submarine

Words and Music by John Lennon and Paul McCartney

Tune down 1/2 step:
(low to high) Eb-Ab-Db-Gb-Bb-Eb

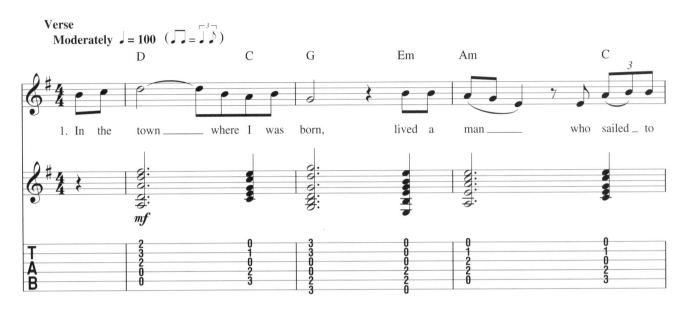

1. In the town _____ where I was born, lived a man _____ who sailed _ to

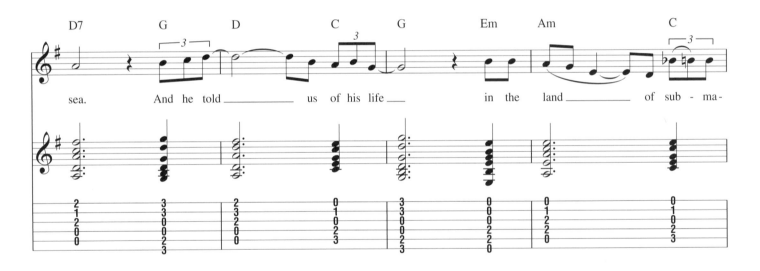

sea. And he told _____ us of his life _____ in the land _____ of sub-ma-

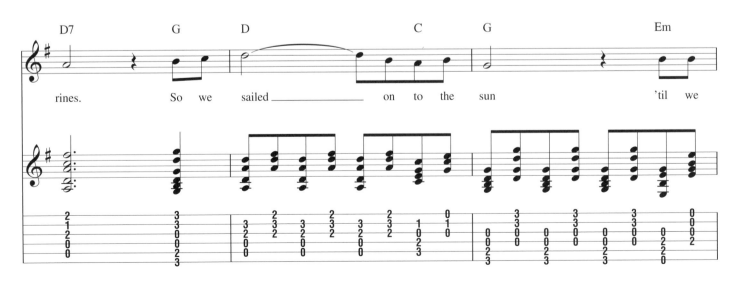

rines. So we sailed _____ on to the sun 'til we

44. JAZZ
I Remember You • I'll Remember April • Impressions • In a Mellow Tone • Moonlight in Vermont • On a Slow Boat to China • Things Ain't What They Used to Be • Yesterdays.
00699689.......................................$14.95

45. TV THEMES
Themes from shows such as: The Addams Family • Hawaii Five-O • King of the Hill • Charlie Brown • Mission: Impossible • The Munsters • The Simpsons • Star Trek®.
00699718.......................................$14.95

46. MAINSTREAM ROCK
Just a Girl • Keep Away • Kryptonite • Lightning Crashes • 1979 • One Step Closer • Scar Tissue • Torn.
00699722.......................................$16.95

47. HENDRIX SMASH HITS
All Along the Watchtower • Can You See Me? • Crosstown Traffic • Fire • Foxey Lady • Hey Joe • Manic Depression • Purple Haze • Red House • Remember • Stone Free • The Wind Cries Mary.
00699723.......................................$19.95

48. AEROSMITH CLASSICS
Back in the Saddle • Draw the Line • Dream On • Last Child • Mama Kin • Same Old Song & Dance • Sweet Emotion • Walk This Way.
00699724.......................................$16.99

49. STEVIE RAY VAUGHAN
Couldn't Stand the Weather • Empty Arms • Lenny • Little Wing • Look at Little Sister • Love Struck Baby • The Sky Is Crying • Tightrope.
00699725.......................................$16.95

50. NÜ METAL
Duality • Here to Stay • In the End • Judith • Nookie • So Cold • Toxicity • Whatever.
00699726.......................................$14.95

51. ALTERNATIVE '90s
Alive • Cherub Rock • Come As You Are • Give It Away • Jane Says • No Excuses • No Rain • Santeria.
00699727.......................................$12.95

52. FUNK
Cissy Strut • Flashlight • Funk #49 • I Just Want to Celebrate • It's Your Thing • Le Freak • Papa's Got a Brand New Bag • Pick up the Pieces.
00699728.......................................$14.95

54. HEAVY METAL
Am I Evil? • Back in Black • Holy Diver • Lights Out • The Trooper • You've Got Another Thing Comin' • The Zoo.
00699730.......................................$14.95

55. POP METAL
Beautiful Girls • Cherry Pie • Get the Funk Out • Here I Go Again • Nothin' but a Good Time • Photograph • Turn up the Radio • We're Not Gonna Take It.
00699731.......................................$14.95

56. FOO FIGHTERS
All My Life • Best of You • DOA • I'll Stick Around • Learn to Fly • Monkey Wrench • My Hero • This Is a Call.
00699749.......................................$14.95

57. SYSTEM OF A DOWN
Aerials • B.Y.O.B. • Chop Suey! • Innervision • Question! • Spiders • Sugar • Toxicity.
00699751.......................................$14.95

58. BLINK-182
Adam's Song • All the Small Things • Dammit • Feeling This • Man Overboard • The Rock Show • Stay Together for the Kids • What's My Age Again?
00699772.......................................$14.95

59. GODSMACK
Awake • Bad Religion • Greed • I Stand Alone • Keep Away • Running Blind • Straight out of Line • Whatever.
00699773.......................................$14.95

60. 3 DOORS DOWN
Away from the Sun • Duck and Run • Here Without You • Kryptonite • Let Me Go • Live for Today • Loser • When I'm Gone.
00699774.......................................$14.95

61. SLIPKNOT
Before I Forget • Duality • The Heretic Anthem • Left Behind • My Plague • Spit It Out • Vermilion • Wait and Bleed.
00699775.......................................$14.95

62. CHRISTMAS CAROLS
God Rest Ye Merry, Gentlemen • Hark! The Herald Angels Sing • It Came upon the Midnight Clear • O Come, All Ye Faithful (Adeste Fideles) • O Holy Night • Silent Night • We Three Kings of Orient Are • What Child Is This?
00699798.......................................$12.95

63. CREEDENCE CLEARWATER REVIVAL
Bad Moon Rising • Born on the Bayou • Down on the Corner • Fortunate Son • Green River • Lodi • Proud Mary • Up Around the Bend.
00699802.......................................$16.99

64. OZZY OSBOURNE
Bark at the Moon • Crazy Train • Flying High Again • Miracle Man • Mr. Crowley • No More Tears • Rock 'N Roll Rebel • Shot in the Dark.
00699803.......................................$16.99

65. THE DOORS
Break on Through to the Other Side • Hello, I Love You (Won't You Tell Me Your Name?) • L.A. Woman • Light My Fire • Love Me Two Times • People Are Strange • Riders on the Storm • Roadhouse Blues.
00699806.......................................$16.99

66. THE ROLLING STONES
Beast of Burden • Happy • It's Only Rock 'N' Roll (But I Like It) • Miss You • Shattered • She's So Cold • Start Me Up • Tumbling Dice.
00699807.......................................$16.95

67. BLACK SABBATH
Black Sabbath • Children of the Grave • Iron Man • N.I.B. • Paranoid • Sabbath, Bloody Sabbath • Sweet Leaf • War Pigs (Interpolating Luke's Wall).
00699808.......................................$16.99

68. PINK FLOYD – DARK SIDE OF THE MOON
Any Colour You Like • Brain Damage • Breathe • Eclipse • Money • Time • Us and Them.
00699809.......................................$16.99

69. ACOUSTIC FAVORITES
Against the Wind • Band on the Run • Free Fallin' • Have You Ever Seen the Rain? • Love the One You're With • Maggie May • Melissa • Mrs. Robinson.
00699810.......................................$14.95

71. CHRISTIAN ROCK
All Around Me • Be My Escape • Come on Back to Me • Hands and Feet • Million Pieces • Strong Tower • Tonight • We Are One Tonight.
00699824.......................................$14.95

72. ACOUSTIC '90s
All Apologies • Daughter • Disarm • Heaven Beside You • My Friends • Name • What I Got • The World I Know.
00699827.......................................$14.95

74. PAUL BALOCHE
Above All • All the Earth Will Sing Your Praises • Because of Your Love • My Reward • Offering • Open the Eyes of My Heart • Praise Adonai • Rise up and Praise Him.
00699831.......................................$14.95

75. TOM PETTY
American Girl • I Won't Back Down • Into the Great Wide Open • Learning to Fly • Mary Jane's Last Dance • Refugee • Runnin' Down a Dream • You Don't Know How It Feels.
00699882.......................................$16.99

76. COUNTRY HITS
Alcohol • Beer for My Horses • Honky Tonk Badonkadonk • It's Five O'Clock Somewhere • Lot of Leavin' Left to Do • Me and My Gang • Pickin' Wildflowers • Summertime.
00699884.......................................$14.95

78. NIRVANA
All Apologies • Come As You Are • Dumb • Heart Shaped Box • In Bloom • Lithium • Rape Me • Smells like Teen Spirit.
00700132.......................................$14.95

88. ACOUSTIC ANTHOLOGY
Don't Ask Me Why • Give a Little Bit • Jack and Diane • The Joker • Midnight Rider • Rocky Raccoon • Walk on the Wild Side • and more.
00700175.......................................$19.95

81. ROCK ANTHOLOGY
Barracuda • Can't Get Enough • Don't Fear the Reaper • Free Ride • Hurts So Good • I Need to Know • Rhiannon • Sultans of Swing • and more.
00700176.......................................$22.99

82. EASY ROCK SONGS
Bad Case of Loving You • Bang a Gong (Get It On) • I Can't Explain • I Love Rock 'N Roll • La Bamba • Mony, Mony • Should I Stay or Should I Go • Twist and Shout.
00700177.......................................$12.99

83. THREE CHORD SONGS
Bye Bye Love • Gloria • I Fought the Law • Love Me Do • Mellow Yellow • Stir It Up • Willie and the Hand Jive • You Don't Mess Around with Jim.
00700178.......................................$12.99

86. BOSTON
Don't Look Back • Long Time • More Than a Feeling • Party • Peace of Mind • Rock & Roll Band • Smokin' • We're Ready.
00700465 ....$16.99

96. THIRD DAY
Blackbird • Call My Name • Consuming Fire • My Hope Is You • Nothing Compares • Tunnel • You Are Mine • Your Love Oh Lord.
00700560.......................................$14.95

97. ROCK BAND
Are You Gonna Be My Girl • Black Hole Sun • Creep • Dani California • In Bloom • Learn to Fly • Say It Ain't So • When You Were Young.
00700703.......................................$14.99

98. ROCK BAND
Ballroom Blitz • Detroit Rock City • Don't Fear the Reaper • Highway Star • Mississippi Queen • Should I Stay or Should I Go • Suffragette City • Train Kept A-Rollin'.
00700704.......................................$14.95